SCHOLASTIC
News
Nonfiction Readers®

This Is the Way We Help at Home

By Amanda Miller

Children's Press®
An Imprint of Scholastic Inc.
New York Toronto London Auckland Sydney
Mexico City New Delhi Hong Kong
Danbury, Connecticut

These content vocabulary word builders are for grades 1–2.

Subject Consultant: Eli J. Lesser, MA, Director of Education, National Constitution Center, Philadelphia, Pennsylvania

Reading Consultant: Cecilia Minden-Cupp, PhD, Early Literacy Consultant and Author, Chapel Hill, North Carolina

Art Direction and Production: Scholastic Classroom Magazines

Library of Congress Cataloging-in-Publication Data

Miller, Amanda.
This is the way we help at home / Amanda Miller.
  p. cm.
Includes bibliographical references and index.
ISBN 13: 978-0-531-21340-7 (lib. bdg.) 978-0-531-21441-1 (pbk.)
ISBN 10: 0-531-21340-4 (lib. bdg.) 0-531-21441-9 (pbk.)
1. Home–Juvenile literature. 2. Family–Juvenile literature. I. Title.
GT2420.M55 2009   640.83–dc22 2009010974

CONTENTS

How Do You Help?

Do you clean up your room?
Do you make your bed?

Kids all around the world do
chores, or jobs at home.
Let's see how they help out.

These children do chores in the United States.

5

Farming and Fishing

These boys live on a **potato** farm. The potatoes grow under the ground.

The boys help their father dig up the potatoes. Later, they eat them for dinner!

potato

These children dig up potatoes in Poland.

It is early in the morning. This boy is already helping his dad!

His father is a **fisherman**. He helps his father put out nets to catch the fish. Then, he goes to school.

fisherman

This boy puts out fishing nets in Greece.

In and Around the Home

Do you ever help out in the kitchen? Many children around the world do.

This boy helps his mom cook dinner. Tonight they are having **noodles**!

noodles

This boy cooks noodles in China.

This girl helps out, too. She gathers **firewood**. First, she looks for wood on the ground. Then, she carries it home on her back.

Her family makes a fire with the wood. They use the fire to cook food.

firewood

This girl gathers firewood in Ethiopia.

Some kids do chores with friends. These children collect water from a well.

They put the water in big **jars**. Then, they carry the jars home on their heads!

They use the water for cooking and washing.

jars

This girl collects water in India.

Animals and Pets

How does this boy help on his family farm? He herds the **llamas**. He helps keep them in one big group.

His parents use the llama hair to make sweaters.

llamas

This boy herds llamas in Peru.

Many kids like this chore best of all. What is it? It is caring for the family pet!

This boy has a pet **wallaby**. He feeds him and plays with him.

How do *you* help out at home?

wallaby

This boy cares for his pet in Australia.

United States

Peru

Greece

Poland

KIDS AROUND THE WORLD

Look at this map. Can you match the children in the photos to the countries where they live?

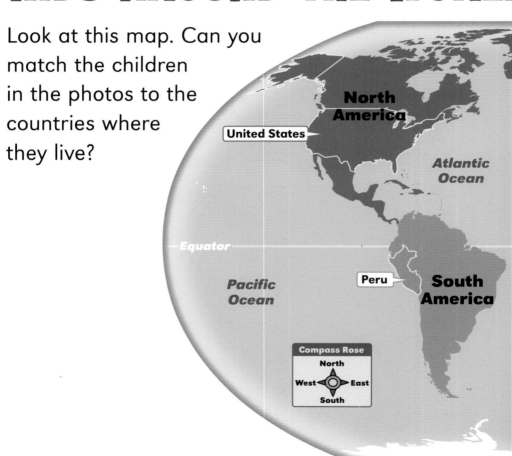

North America

United States

Atlantic Ocean

Equator

Pacific Ocean

Peru

South America

Compass Rose
North
West — East
South

Ethiopia

China

India

Australia

HELP AT HOME

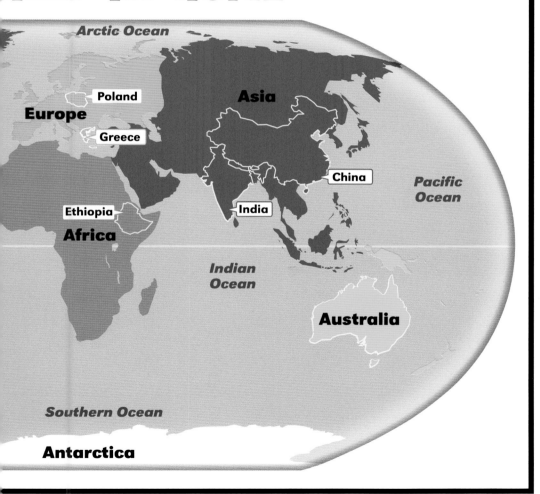

Arctic Ocean

Europe

Poland

Greece

Asia

China

India

Pacific Ocean

Ethiopia

Africa

Indian Ocean

Australia

Southern Ocean

Antarctica

YOUR NEW WORDS

chores (chorz) jobs that have to been done regularly

firewood (**fire**-wud) pieces of wood that can be burned to make heat or for cooking

fisherman (**fish**-ur-muhn) someone who catches fish as a job or for fun

jars (jarz) containers with wide mouths

llamas (**lah**-muhz) large animals from South America that are used for wool and to carry things

noodles (**noo**-duhlz) flat strips of dough that are cooked and eaten

potato (puh-**tay**-toh) the underground part of a leafy plant, that is eaten in many countries

wallaby (**wol**-uh-bee) an animal from Australia that is like a kangaroo but smaller

INDEX

FIND OUT MORE

Book:

Kindersley, Anabel and Kindersley, Barnabas. *Children Just Like Me*. New York: DK Children, 1995.

Website:

PBS Kids
http://pbskids.org/itsmylife/family/index.html

MEET THE AUTHOR

Amanda Miller is a writer and editor for Scholastic. She and her dog, Henry, live in Brooklyn, New York. When she was younger, her favorite chore was cutting the grass.